F*ck Motivation: It's your Life

A Guide on How to Live your Life and Be Happy

Other Books by R and R

Meditation for beginners
What is Meditation and how can it change your life? A Guide to mindfulness and happiness.

F*ck Motivation
It's your life. A guide on how to live your life and be happy.

Declutter
A beginners 10 step guide on how to simplify life by decluttering.

New Habits - New Wealth
How changing some habits can improve your personal health and financial wealth.

Puppy Training
Top 10 ideas for training your dog within a month to keep everybody in your house happy and stress free.

Minimalist
The How-To and Why of becoming a minimalist

www.randrdigitallifestyle.com

Table of Contents

Introduction

Have you ever been left wondering what successful people do differently than others? What makes their lives so unique? Why can't your life be every bit as happy as theirs? The fact is that it can, but you just haven't taken the leap of faith yet. In this book, we will show you what's missing from your particular equation, so that you can get your life on track and instantly feel inclined toward doing what it takes.

You may be surprised that you have more control over your life than you think. We have heard people who have come to us for advice moaning about why their lives are so bad, but when push comes to shove, the only person who needed shoving in the right direction was them! That's why we wrote this book. They actually begged us to because our system works, and it can be your system too. It's all about the Law of Attraction and getting rid of all of the negativity that you allow to get in the way of your progress. Yes, it's you who allows it. Thus, we need to teach you a new way to look at life that not only gives you the incentive to succeed and be happy, but that will lead you to do the things you need to do without having to motivate yourself. As the title says, "F*ck Motivation!" You don't need motivational books to tell you what you already know.

What you do need is a step in the right direction, followed by another step in the right direction. Once we help you to find that direction, you won't look back with regret anymore. In fact, you will have so many ideas about where your life is going that you will be tireless! Read on and find your energy within the pages of this book. Once you have, don't forget where you got that sense of happiness from. Be prepared to congratulate yourself because you are the only one who can make this kind of difference to your own life!

Chapter One

Learn not to Listen to Naysayers

Do you know what a naysayer is? These are people you allow to influence your life. From the moment that you walk and talk, there are people within your life who decide where the boundaries of proper behavior come from. Your parents, your siblings, people who don't believe in what you believe in are going to tell you that you cannot succeed. Unfortunately, their influence on you is more significant than you may think. When you have been in a relationship of any kind that held you back, you will carry with you all of the negative impacts that these naysayers may have on your life.

Let us give you an example. Kayleigh wanted to be an artist. She had the talent, and she absolutely loved what she was capable of doing, though, over the years, family and friends had dissuaded her from doing what made her happy. She took up an accounting job because they wanted her to have financial security. The truth is that they didn't have her kind of creativity and could not imagine her being able to make a decent living as an artist. Traditional social standards see artists as being poor people who scrape a living.

She married and was reasonably happy with her life, but then one night came home from exercise class to find her husband keeping fit with her best friend. You don't have to wait for moments like this for the light bulb to come on. Unfortunately, in Kayleigh's case, she was affected by it and ended up having a nervous breakdown. During the time that she spent in a mental health facility, she examined what it was that she was feeling and where she wanted to go from that moment on.

She had done everything according to the wishes of the naysayers, and now she found she was at a juncture in her life when she wasn't prepared to ignore her own passions anymore in favor of those imposed upon her. Her mother had died, and her father was utterly miserable in his life, and she was determined that it was not how she wanted to be in her advancing years.

Kayleigh went back to her art. Yes, it meant giving up a career, but she didn't do it in a manner that meant she had to start from nothing. Kayleigh just gave less time to work and more time to her passion. Instead of living to work, she used work to pay for all of the things that she wanted to do, and this led her toward the success that she had always craved as a professional artist. It took time, but once she had learned where she wanted her life to go, it became easier for her. The lessons that can be learned from this experience are simple:

- Know the direction you want to go in

- Have a long term plan

- Don't listen to those who don't believe in your dreams

- Work toward those dreams in a realistic way

So how do you work out where you want to go in your life? We have asked people who come to us for advice to outline what their dream is, and many don't actually have any firm goals. "I want to be rich" doesn't cut it. How rich? You have to quantify what it is that you want because, without this qualification, you don't have a specific destination and cannot possibly work toward a goal that keeps moving.

The next thing to ask yourself is what you want to do with your life that will make you feel fulfilled and happy. People don't know what happiness is until they experience it, so once again, it's hard to qualify. However, there will be strengths within your character that you know you can work on to go forward toward success and you need to hone in on these and then make yourself an ideas chart so that you can add ideas that will become part of your everyday activities and that work toward you being where you want to be.

Kayleigh did this and made lists of jobs that allowed her to be artistic, and it was from this list that she eventually found her niche. Writers have niches, but so do people from all different types of jobs, and once you know what your particular niche is, you can use that to explore what possibilities there are that include your passions as a means of making a living. You may have seen on the TV people who go abroad to work, but many of these do this to find themselves and are then disappointed that they don't actually change in character. They change location but live the same kind of lives abroad as they would be faced with living at home. The difference is that if you already know what your passions are, you can work toward including these within your life even though you may be forced to do work you don't particularly like to get there! If that's all it is and it's a means to an end, you don't mind so much because you know that the mundane work that you are forced to do is working toward something your heart wants to do.

Now work out who the naysayers are in your life

Naysayers are people who don't believe in you. These can be people from your family, friends who are always negative about your hopes and dreams, or people within your workplace. You need to let go of negative influence, although some people can't be cut out of your life that easily. In these cases, know who they are and cut down your contact with them, preferring to be with people who believe in you and share your hopes and dreams. You are limiting the amount of negative impact people have on you while you work toward doing whatever it is that you want to do in your life. That means that at the end of the day, you don't need their approval. You can find your way and work out what makes you happy. Sara wanted to be a writer. She never found the time, and there are millions of would-be writers held back by naysayers and using the excuse that they don't have time in their lives. If you believe in something and distance yourself from people who are naysayers, you will find the time, as Sara did when she published her first book. She didn't know what a following she would get, but her sister, who had disapproved of her choice to become a writer was actually jealous of her lifestyle later in their lives and when it came to retirement, didn't know what she would do with her life. The difference? Sara's life didn't stop at retirement, and in fact, she didn't foresee retirement since what she had chosen to do for a living was her passion.

Naysayers come in all kinds of disguises. For the next week, observe people and when you find time on your own, go through the influences in your life and work out which of these dissuades you from doing what you want to do. You need all the support that you can get when seeking happiness and fulfillment, so negative influences aren't going to help you. We remember once watching a program about a cleaning lady. The movie showed how her happiness lay in buying a stylish dress from Dior. Her life would never allow her to wear something like this, but she didn't let the naysayers stop her from putting aside a little of her money each week until she had enough for a dress from the fashion house in Paris. When you believe in your dreams, no one can stop you from fulfilling them

UNLESS you let them. You may say "But I have to earn a living!" and of course you do, but you don't have to make it drudgery. Make it a means to an end like Mrs. Harris did, and you fulfill those dreams. She actually looked amazing in her Dior dress, and if that's what made her happy, no one had the right to be a naysayer in her life and stop that situation from occurring.

Naysayers will always hold you back IF YOU LET THEM. You have to use your own common sense to work out the scenario in your life where your dreams can be included. You don't have to stop being you, just because you don't fit into a particular mold presented to you by these very Naysayers who just love to make people feel their opinions are essential. They are not. As you move through the chapters of this book, expect to come back and look over each chapter, because you have some work to do for yourself. You may get away with merely reading for the time being, but the exercises in each chapter are there to help you to find realization all on your own.

Chapter Two

Don't be a Follower

Do you have any idea what a follower is? Well, let us tell you. A follower is someone who sees something in a magazine and feels like they need to copy the ideas in order to conform to society standards. They worry about other people's perceptions of them, and these could be genuine concerns of someone who is a follower:

- I am not the shape that I need to be

- I need to be married by a specific date

- I need to have children by a certain age

- I need to have a huge home and car

- I need all of the material trappings that life offers me

The fact is that when you are in your coffin, no one is going to look back on your life and make comments like this:

- Wow, she was a great shape

- Wow, she was sensible and married by 25

- Wow, she left it too late to have kids

- Wow, she had the biggest home in the street

At the end of the day, none of these things matter. Authenticity is the name of the game and what that means is being true to who you are. You don't need to go along with ideas simply because you don't seem to have any of your own for the time being. The reason that you don't have unique ideas about what you want to do with your life is because you have let the media have far too much of your time and are highly influenced by it. Does it matter that you don't have flawless skin or that you don't have the muscles that others do? Of course not, so stop being a follower! Start to lead your own life, and in the process, you will find that it leads you to the place you want to be. Following others will never help you. It merely imposes boundaries, and you may find that you don't need those boundaries. They may be limiting you and stopping you from finding out what's right for you. Accept yourself for who you are and learn to be happy with it. Do you really think all your Facebook friends are as happy as they portray themselves to be? If they really posted photos of what their real lives were like, you would probably be surprised. You are not the only one with ambitions and dreams, and they certainly haven't found theirs yet because they are spending all their time on Facebook dreams. Learn the reality of your life and stop being a follower of fashions and ideas that are someone else's.

Chapter Three

Why Analysis Paralysis Doesn't Work

In the world that we are living in, we are continually being thrown ideas. You watch TV, you may read Twitter, and you may even take notice of what your friends are doing on Facebook. Then, you may also have a Kindle or watch movies on your phone. The fact is that your mind is being invaded in all directions, and it's not actually making you a much happier person. You are being overloaded. If you haven't heard about stepping off the roundabout and into Zen, then it would be rare in this day and age. People are trying to find themselves, and I don't blame them. Our society is lost and can't seem to find its direction and when you look to see why it becomes self-evident indeed.

We surround ourselves with "stuff," and we make friends quickly with strangers that we will never meet. We base our lives upon what we own instead of who we are and how many followers we have instead of being content to be ourselves and let nature take its course. Look around you, and you will also see that you are sitting here analyzing your life and that the reason you bought this book in the first place is probably that you want to examine your life even further. We have bad news for you. It is not our intention to get you to analyze because you paralyze your imagination by doing so. Look around you:

- Decide what is essential to your life
- Decide what gives pleasure to your life
- Decide what is superfluous to your life
- Get rid of distractions
- Switch your phone off when you don't need it
- Switch off your alerts
- Stop being at everyone's beck and call

Now start to breathe, and we mean really breathe. You will probably laugh at this notion because you have to know how to breathe to actually live. However, there's a different kind of breathing. This is deep breathing that helps your sympathetic nervous system to be able to do all the jobs that it has to do in your body. Breathe in and count at the same time. When you get to 8 breathe out and when you get to ten start again. If you can do this in a quiet place with absolutely no distractions, for 15 to 20 minutes a day, you will find that you start to simplify your thought processes. Why? The subconscious mind has a habit of jumping in and making assumptions about your life based on your past performance. This new type of breathing is accompanied by letting go of thoughts and if they come, acknowledging them and then telling them that they are not appropriate at this time. What you are doing is putting it all into slow motion so that your subconscious mind sees your response to life as calm and lacking in any kind of judgment. That's good stuff. More information on this type of techniques can be found in <u>Meditation For Beginners.</u>

You see, when you spend all of your time being surrounded by media and then add to this all of the thoughts that you have in a day, a large percentage of those thoughts are unnecessary and muddle the whole picture because there is too much overload. Your mind cannot deal with it. Analysis paralysis is very real. Let us show you an example if you don't believe me. Repeat the word "tangling" over and over again out loud, and within five minutes, the word will have no sense anymore. Unless it's in context, it's just sounds coming from your body. Well, overload of analysis is precisely the same. You give yourself all of this information that you don't actually need to succeed. Let go of it even if just for a short while each day, and you will see that clarity becomes part of your life and that you can see problems from a much clearer viewpoint.

The other thing that you need to remember is that the brain isn't capable of multi-tasking, although every day you overload it with analysis and questions, it also has to cope with everything that's going on around you, and there is little wonder that your analysis turns into gobbledygook. It's bound to happen. By distancing yourself from life a little sometimes, you improve your motivation, and you don't do things because others want you to. You do them because you can, and those things that people are good at and excel at are those they enjoy enough to do without any kind of motivation!

If you let go of the analysis and just start living your life in this moment, you find a happiness you really didn't know was there, although it was all the time. It's not going to point itself out to you if your mind is filled with rubbish. You won't see it, and you won't enjoy it. If, however, you rest your mind and find the spiritual person within yourself, then you don't have to look for inspiration. It is all around you. People often ask us where we get our enthusiasm for life from, but it's easy. We learned a very long time ago that analysis paralysis kills off creativity, and when you let go of it, you begin to find what's really important to you.

So do take about fifteen minutes each morning and make "breathing practice" a part of your life. If you find that anything interrupts you, then choose a better spot the next day. Your mind needs to be in the here and now sometimes and when you pull it back through all the knots that have formed in your mind, analysis paralysis won't stop you from achieving everything that you set out to do. In fact, your mind will see in such great clarity that you may even find yourself doing the breathing exercises before important meetings or interviews, or may use it to escape the hubbub of everyday life.

Chapter Four

Looking for Approval from Others

When you are a baby, and you take your first steps, the people around you cheer and clap and give you validation. You have done something well. However, in your life as an adult, you don't need that validation. If you do, then you need to look at your self-esteem levels because if you rely on others to validate you, you are going about it all the wrong way. It makes you weak. It makes you unhappy, and it makes you feel weaker every time you don't get that validation. Can't you see the hole that you are digging for yourself?

Graham was always looking for approval. He needed it because he didn't have faith in himself. After difficult relationships, Graham found himself questioning his life to such an extent that he needed other people to approve of what he did. He was always unhappy. These are the kind of questions he found himself asking others:

- Was that a nice evening?

- Did you enjoy yourself?

- Did I get you the right gift?

It took a long while for Graham to realize what he was doing. He was making up for his own personal shortfall by getting other people to praise him. That was what he saw as a boost, but when we explained to him how false that was, it took him a while to realize how true that was. What happened when people didn't validate him? What happened when he did things that people didn't approve of? He thought about it for a moment and then sadly admitted that he had made his life about what other people thought because he couldn't face the failure that he saw himself as.

Many people feel that way, and they need to get back to their roots and find out what they want to do with their lives instead of perpetuating this awful habit. All it did was make them feel good for a few minutes, and then they were needy again. We explained all of this to Graham and asked him to go through a whole day with a happy heart greeting people with a smile but not asking for their approval. His subconscious mind saw that as being his response to life and instantly kicked in when something happened, but he had to stem this habit. So, we gave him another habit to hold onto when this happened. Instead of asking someone else's approval for something he had done, we taught him to approve of himself. Instead of begging for other people to approve, we taught him to treat himself to something nice when he approved of something he did. It's easy when you change a habit but be aware that you need to keep it up for about 40 days before it becomes a habit.

If you act like someone who can't survive without other people's approval, you become someone who can't survive without other people's approval, just like Graham had become. When he changed the habit and started to pat himself on the back for what he had done, he began to attract more positive people into his life and didn't wake up each morning dreading another day. He found the incentive to do well because he liked the feeling of doing well. It didn't matter if others approved or not. The feeling inside him grew into a self-liking, and when you like yourself, you gain friendships that are worth having and respect from people around you.

What's that got to do with motivation and happiness? Well, people try so hard to motivate themselves when all they have to do is please that one person that matters the most – themselves. The way that you are dictates what happens to you in your life. Poor men who always give the impression they are the underdogs remain the underdogs because they don't know how to be anything else. People mold themselves to roles, and that's where they go wrong. If you mold yourself to the role you want in life, then you will become that person, and everything that you do will be geared toward becoming that person. You won't have problems because all of your mental energies attract energies on a similar level.

Happiness comes from accepting who you are and knowing where you are going to go in life without having to lean on others or obey what they feel is best for you. Stop lying down and letting people wipe their feet on you. Effectively, that's what you are doing when you depend on others for their approval. It's up to them how dirty the doormat gets, and sometimes when they don't approve of you, that mat can get pretty grubby. However, if you use the gage that you need to approve of yourself, you don't have to worry about being a doormat anymore and being dependent upon the grace of others to make you feel validated.

For the exercise for this chapter, we would suggest that you write down the things that you want to do tomorrow. Make the list doable and then just do it, but make sure that you have equal amounts of work, rest, and play. You are entitled to all of these. The work could be the work that you do every day to pay your bills. The rest could be breaks when things get tough, and the play could be rewarding yourself because you are worth it. You don't need to be approved of by others. Imagine if Bill Gates had taken great stock of other people's opinions. The first bank manager he asked for backing from actually refused him, but it didn't make him lie down and become the banker's doormat. Believe in what you do and don't ask for other people's approval. Approve of yourself and start to liberate yourself from being a victim of the way other people decide to treat you.

Chapter Five

It's your Life!

You must have heard people say this to you a million times, but how many times have you given the words "it's your life" any deep and meaningful thought? The problem that many people face is that they go through their lives, bending who they are to suit others. We remember talking to a widow. She had been married for 40 years, and when her husband passed away, she suddenly found that the person she was wasn't the person she used to be. Somewhere along those forty years, she had bent the person she was into what her husband wanted her to be. The problem with this way of thinking is that he probably didn't want her to change at all. He loved her when he met her initially, but what happens is that we create ideas in our minds about what we need to do to be the perfect spouse and she had done all of those things, but now she was left with someone she no longer knew.

Looking back through the photographs of her life was a joy, but it could have been a bigger joy. Among all of the pictures of people having a good time stood a woman with a camera that never really stepped into the limelight. No one really photographed her. Then she looked at her courtship photographs and the photographs of her wedding and started to remember little bits of who she was at that time. The problem with life is that it is ever-changing. You can never take for granted your circumstances. They change, but the person who has to go through those circumstances will still be the same person physically. She wanted to chase dreams again and suddenly realized that the TV shows she watched were chosen by her husband. The music she listened to was equally his choice, so she went on a mission. Going through every aspect of her life, she decided that those things that were not authentically her had to go. Of course, she kept mementos of things that had been landmarks in her life, but now she felt a new sense of purpose and was able to follow her dreams. If you want to start decluttering every aspect of your life, you can read Declutter to help you with the process.

The great thing is that when you choose the right person, and you refuse to compromise on who you are, you may find that this is just the person your partner loves and respects. Authenticity has a lot to do with happiness, and you do only get one chance at it. Thus, you need to make that chance in life work for you, for the people you love and for the greater harmony of the world that you live in. The way to do this is to ask yourself who accepts you the way you really are? These are the best friends to have. If you have friends who criticize you at the slightest thing, then ask yourself whether these people contribute enough to your life to stay in it. Since life is a precious gift, you need to embrace it and to do that, this means being authentic and being with people who love your authenticity. Their approval isn't paramount to your existence, and it isn't conditional, but when you find those people who add to your life, grab them with both hands and enjoy them. Those who don't want to accept you for who you are, need to find their own friendships, as you don't have enough time in your life for them to waste it.

The average lifespan of an American is 78.69 years. That seems a hell of a lot when you are young, but as you get older, it shrinks. The point we want to make is that you only have a set amount of time in which to be happy. If you're going to spend it being miserable and stressed, then that's your business, but it isn't the wisest way to go. There are those who drown themselves in minor ailments that turn into more significant illnesses. "I have this...." says one lady who is grossly overweight and never exercises. "I think I may have this...." says another who is looking for an excuse not to do the painting he promised his wife he would do. We go through our lives making excuses for our own shortcomings, and that's sad because all of these years are wasted. Add to this the fact that you may get run over by a hit and run driver tomorrow, and you need to ask yourself, "What did my life stand for?" It doesn't have to stand for much, but the least you can expect from your life is that you are permitted to be authentic and that you don't have to go through life trying to be something you are not.

It's your life, and you need to greet each morning with gratitude for all the good things that you have in your life. Whether you believe in a maker or not is up to you. Sometimes we need to gather perspective, and if you want to experience true happiness, you have to get back to basics and find humility. How can it help? Well, when you have a humble approach to life, your expectations are less, and you tend to fulfill what it is that you set out to do. In these days, doctors and scientists are working out that mindfulness is helping so many people and all this means is being mindful of the things that you do in your life. For example, do you sit and eat your food and really taste every texture and flavor? Do you really look at all the wonders of nature?

To get the perspective back in your life, we want you to choose a place that you know that takes your breath away. It could be a beach at sunset or sunrise. It could be a hill where you can see all of the countryside around you. It just has to be natural, and it has to be somewhere that awes you. There was a beach where we used to go to get this perspective back, and at sunset, it was amazing. What nature does is remind you of how small you are. Why would you want to be small? Well, the world is made up of millions of smaller bits and pieces that give it value, and you are just one of them. When you feel this oneness, it helps you to take a kinder stance on life and upon yourself. You greet the world with gratitude, and you are happier within yourself.

This also helps you to appreciate each day and to see it for what it is – i.e., an opportunity to work toward your dreams. Your life is a dream catcher, and if you blow on it too hard, it can't catch the dreams or make them a reality. If you take it slowly, but according to your OWN PLAN, then you get to places you never dreamed of. Our bucket list keeps changing. Why? Because on it, we keep all the things we want to do and these are not humongous feats. They are simply steps toward where we eventually want to be. We don't neglect good friendships.

We trust ourselves and have won the trust of others. We are happy in our own skin, and that's where you need to get yourself. Little by little, the bucket list becomes a reality, and it can be updated. As you achieve one goal and celebrate it, go for another. The world is really out there waiting for you to discover it. We could give you so many examples of how people's lives have been turned around when they stop trying so damned hard to live up to other people's expectations. Georgia was pressured by her parents to have a baby. The more she tried, the less it happened, until one day, she told her parents that although she loved them, she wasn't prepared to live a life of disappointment because she couldn't do what they wanted her to do. Strangely enough, when Georgia stopped trying, she enjoyed sex a lot more and actually conceived!

You need to decide on your own priorities. It's not someone else's life. It's yours. There are no guarantees in this life. There are kids in the world who have no drinking water and others that spend all day fretting about the color of their nail polish or the shape of their lips. Come on now. Grow up and see that life is too beautiful to waste and that you have so many things to be happy about. Sadness doesn't become anyone. It's ugly and un-welcomed by most people. When you learn to make happiness your most important facet, the rest follows, and it gives you all of the strength that you need to face all the hardships of life because you are stronger. You need to think about the fact that the kids in the next room are joyful, rather than seeing them as a nuisance. Soon, they will be gone. The cycle of life is something you can't change. You can't rule other people's lives, but you have so much power over how yours pans out.

Start a gratitude diary and in the front of it, write down all the things that you are thankful for. In the back, keep a list of things that you feel you want to do this week, this year, in your lifetime. When you know the road you want to take in life, everything becomes so much clearer, and you succeed without really having to put in too much effort at all. The reason for this is because you have a plan and all of the things that you do in your everyday life lead you toward achieving that plan. That's all that life is. A period of 78.96 years that can be filled with joy or that you can throw in the gutter. The choice is yours. It's your life.

Chapter Six

Taking Action Regardless of Past Experiences

I heard Kelly tell her mom that she couldn't swim. That was years ago, and now Kelly is all grown up and didn't let her failure as a child get in the way of learning something new. On her own terms, in her own time, she learned to swim and goes swimming every week. The fact is that we look back on our past failures and use these as excuses for not trying something again. Look at the statements below:

- I can't wear clothes like that
- I can't face her
- I can't get onto a plane
- I can't walk that far

The point of this chapter is that your life begins today. It doesn't matter what failures you have had in the past. Perhaps it isn't even crucial for you to achieve the things that you failed at in the past. However, you should never let that feeling of failure follow you through your life. As well as the years that are passing, something fundamental is happening to you as an individual. You are changing as you get older. You are also getting more afraid of life because of past experiences, and this has to stop. You are not the sum total of your failures. You are the sum total of everything that you are in this moment. Thus, you need to make each moment count as much as you can.

Did you say that you loved your partner after that huge row? Did you tell your child it is okay not to be on the sports team? Did you let a friend know that you were thinking of her? No? Well, today it all starts over. You get a chance to wake up to the world and do the things that you know you should be doing. In the case of a child, that child needs support and encouragement. In the case of a friend, the friend is one who gives and takes in equal measure and sometimes a surprise phone call can make her day a little bit brighter. What about the things that you wanted to learn but never got around to? If you take baby steps toward achieving them, you can do anything. For example, if you want to learn to swim, you first need to make an appointment for private swimming lessons. That first step toward doing anything in your life changes the whole dynamic of your life. Ruby, for example, wanted to leap out of an aircraft. Once she had made the appointment, she was thrilled not only that she had the experience to look forward to but that she'd been brave enough to actually step over barriers and make that dream available to herself.

If you are constantly reminded of your failures, it's time to change. Write down those perceived failures and then rip the paper into tiny pieces, because who you were when you made those mistakes is not who you are today. Today you are a new person, who has decided to try new things and to make those things a part of his/her new life. From learning to knit right through the spectrum to taking an examination to help you to become a surgeon, all things are possible, but you need to take all of the steps toward doing them that you haven't taken before. If you want a little push in the right direction, tell an excellent close friend what you are doing, and they will encourage you to follow through. Some people don't have confidence in themselves to fulfill their dreams, and sometimes that little push from a friend can make all of the difference.

Sometimes small actions begin the journey into the unknown. For example, John always wanted to try calligraphy but never really got around to it. He also wanted to learn to play the guitar. As soon as opportunity put a guitar within affordable reach, John started to make plans to have basic lessons to learn the chords. With calligraphy, he bought the paper and the calligraphy pens and began to make scrolls for gifts for friends and got better and better at it by watching YouTube videos. Even though John had no real artistic talent, John actually enjoyed producing something that people would frame and treasure. John talked about having tried calligraphy in his youth and it was a half-hearted attempt, and he wasn't very good at it, but you don't need artistic talent to actually produce great work. If you don't have artistic talent, there are loads of people who offer you designs on the Internet and show you how to create them. John didn't let his old experiences get in the way of learning new things. Small actions lead you toward where you want to be. You have to take that leap of faith and just decide what those things are.

Our advice to you is to write yourself a list of things you want to achieve in your life. These can be short term plans, vacations you want to take or new things that you want to learn. Remember, what happened to you in the past does not dictate your future. Let us explain this in a very emotional case, which demonstrates it perfectly. Lara was raped as a teen. She went through her life, carrying that scar with her, and it made her feel insignificant and unheard. It also affected her relationships with others because Lara felt that the experience made her into less of a person than she was before. Logic will tell you that a rape victim is not to blame, but she didn't see it in this way for a very long time. When Lara heard singing outside a church one winter's evening, she found herself drawn toward it. She sang as well, and it was recognized that she had the voice of an angel. The church invited her to join the choir, and that started a chance journey into finding faith in herself. Now married with two children and living a very happy life, she learned that she was not the sum total of her experiences, but that her experiences had given her a strength that she would not have had without that experience. You can't write off the past. It happened. But there's no need to live it.

The best way of explaining this is mindfulness. It teaches you that the moment that you are in is the beginning. This moment counts at this time, and what happened in the past should be left there. All of the time that you spend in retrospective thought, you are not living in this moment at all, and you may as well lie down and die. Really! You are stepping back into that experience and not allowing yourself the wonders of now.

Similarly, people who spend today worrying about tomorrow are wasting the opportunities that are offered today. They don't notice that the first flowers of spring are appearing from the ground because their thoughts are firmly on the exam they have to take tomorrow. Perhaps there wasn't much money for food today, and they worry about what they will eat tomorrow, but the fact is that while their minds are on tomorrow, they cannot actually enjoy the food that is set out on the table in front of them.

Stop for a moment, and simply look around you. There is so much in this moment and all of your burdens from the past need to be left behind. You can win. You can find happiness, and you can walk toward your dreams, but only if you decide to empty your mind of all judgment of others and thoughts of past or future. Now is all that you have and you need to make it count. Even when you have mundane tasks to do, concentrate on them, and get them done quicker. Stop allowing yourself to find reasons not to live the life that you have in the time that you have. Once you learn to do that, you let go of perceptions such as "What if....?" Life improves once you can do that, so make it something you do from this moment. Use all of your senses to enjoy the day that you have and move toward a brighter future.

There are no excuses for apathy. The past is not a reflection of who you are right now. Be aware of the person that you are now and enjoy it to the fullest. With each passing day, you are getting older, and instead of treating each day with indifference or dread, greet it with gratitude. You are still here, still walking toward an unknown future, but knowing that you can have some say in shaping that future. Only then will you find true peace of mind and the happiness that everyone deserves to experience in their lifetimes.

We promised you solutions, but we can't make you take those suggestions and make them actionable in your life. YOU have to do that. We would suggest reading over the chapters again and taking the actions suggested to see if they make a difference in your life. We know that they will, but you have to have the will to find happiness. After you do, you won't be looking for motivation because it will be all around you, offering you the happiness everyone should have in their lives. It's yours for the taking, once you learn the approach and decide that's the path that you are on.

Conclusion

We have come to the end of this book too soon. There is so much to share about life that a small volume cannot really do it justice. However, the ideas that we have suggested will make a massive difference in your life. There are so many people in life who try to hold you back for their own motives. Your parents give you advice because they want what they see as best for you. It's their protective instincts, although if you asked them, they would probably admit to the adult you that they didn't know what they were doing as parents and just muddled on in the best way they knew. Those naysayers may have had honorable reasons, but you now need to work out who they are and what's actually true in your own life. Make your own decisions and don't let others use you as their doormat.

For just one moment, after having read this book, close your eyes and see what makes you happy. Look at the colors of happiness and feel the sensation of happiness. It's all inside you, and you don't need to analyze it. Remember what we said about overthinking something. Try this. Smile at the next person you see in the street and look how happiness spreads. Forget about over-analyzing anything because it only leads to a state of mind that is confusing and that cripples your creativity.

In one chapter, we mentioned about approval from others. We all try to get this from school days. Being the most popular kid on the block matters when you are a child, but when you take this need to please into adulthood, you put other people's needs before your own and find that you need their approval. Forget it. Do something just because you want to do it without any thanks from anyone and see how it makes you feel inside. Give the neighbor some of your crops or bake a cake and give it away for the sake of making someone around you a little happier. Don't do it for approval or thanks because when you do that, you set yourself up for disappointment.

There was a point in the book when we mentioned about this being your life. Go back to that chapter and read it again and again until you are sure that the information has sunk in. The problem is that the longer you put off living, the faster your life is gone. It's not infinite. It's a set number of years in which you have all the chance in the world to find happiness. Drown out the negativity and start to live your life.

We hope that this book has been of use to you and that you have found something within our pearls of wisdom that hit home. We are not gurus, but we have learned from the best. Everything in your life starts inside you. Bitterness and unhappiness do as well. Once you realize your own personal power over your sense of happiness, you can live the life of your dreams and find that state that people call "happy." It isn't about motivation at all, so f*ck that! It's about letting life give you the opportunity to shine and wanting to.

Thank you for reading to the end of the book – R & R

Please leave feedback for this book on Amazon – Cheers – Ray & Ruby

www.ingramcontent.com/pod-product-compliance
Lightning Source LLC
Chambersburg PA
CBHW071756020426
42331CB00008B/2314